Real Estate Script Book

Excelleum Coaching & Consulting

By
Debbie De Grote

Anderson-Noble Publishing
Long Beach, California

Copyright © MMXIV by Debbie De Grote.

All Rights reserved. No part of this publication may be reproduced or transmitted in any form or by any means electronic or mechanical, including photocopy, recording, or any information storage and retrieval system now know or to be invented, without permission in writing from the publisher, except by a reviewer who wishes to quote brief passages in connection with a review written for inclusion in a magazine, newspaper, or broadcast. Published by Anderson – Noble Publishing, 12340 Seal Beach Blvd., #B632, Seal Beach, CA 90740. Second edition.

Visit our Web site at **www.Excelleum.com** for more information on Debbie De Grote.

Library of Congress Control Number: 2015947204

ISBN: 978-0-9842827-6-0

Published in the United States of America by
Big Guns Marketing, LLC dba
Anderson – Noble Publishing
12340 Seal Beach Blvd., #B632
Seal Beach, CA 90740

Excelleum…When Excellence Matters

This book is available at quantity discounts for bulk purchases.
For information, please call 1-855-420-140

Table of Contents

Introduction 3
How to Practice 4-5
Key Communication Reminders 6-8
Listing Process- Prequalify 9
Setting a Listing Appointment and Prequalification Worksheet 10-11
Script to Set up the Prequalification 12
Assumptive Technique Script 13
Send Pre-appointment Package 14
Script to Prepare them for the Pre-appointment Package..14
Script to be the Last Interviewed in a Multiple Interview 15-16
Verbal Suggestion Script 17
Listing Script at the Table 18
Script to Review Market Evaluation..19
Handling Objections 20-22
Objections at the Listing 23-25
Things to Think About Before Taking an Overpriced Listing 26
The Listing Process Continued 27-29
Themes for Seller Calls 30-31
Additional Listing Process Objections..32-33
Script to Obtain First Price Reduction 34
Price Reduction Objections 35
Negotiating Offers with the Seller 36-37
Buyer Objections 38-41
Past Clients and Sphere of Influence Script 42-43
Script for Calling Past Clients/ When it has been a Long Time Since You Called.........................44
Script for Lead Follow Up 45-46
Script for Asking for Referrals in Social Situations 47-48
Script for Inside Sales Person Calling to Call Your Database 49
Script for the Administrative Team to Ask for Referrals 50
Script to Ask Your Vendors for Referrals 51
Script to Ask New Sellers for Referrals 52
Script for Asking a Buyer for a Referral at the First Appointment 53
Script for Cold Calling/ Calling around Listings or Sales 54
Cold Calling Objections 55-56
Script for Doorknocking/ Cold Calling/ Farming 57
Script for Telemarketer Cold Calling 58
Script and Approach at an Open House 59-60
Script for Calling Absentee Owners 61-62
Script for Talking to Renters 63

- Script for Expireds 64-66
- Expired Objections 67-71
- Script for the FSBO 72-73
- Script for New Buyer Agent When Calling FSBO 74-75
- Effective FSBO Follow Up 76
- FSBO Objections 77-80
- Script to Thank Customer After Closing 81
- Script for Asking a Buyer to Work Exclusively with You 82
- Script for Asking a Buyer to Start the Pre-Approval Process 83
- Great FSBO Questions 84-85
- Great Questions to Ask Expireds and Old Expireds 86
- Resort Script 87
- Promise Technique 88

Welcome to the First Edition of the Excelleum Real Estate Script Book!

In this book, I have attempted to cover most of the common real estate scripts that you will likely need. If there is one that I have not included, email me and I will create it for you and add it to the next edition of our book.

Before we begin, let's take a minute to talk about why scripts are so important. **You see, your words do matter!** Often I will hear salespeople say, "Oh, I don't need a script; I like to wing it," or "I don't like canned presentations."

If they would really be honest with themselves, they would discover that they do have scripts (things they often say); however, what they say may not be as powerful as it could be.

> If you are looking to be more powerful and confident, and to produce consistent and predictable results, then you need scripts!
>
> If you want to be free of worrying about what you will say next and be able to listen, focus on the customer, and put your efforts into building trust and rapport, then you need scripts!
>
> If you want to do well, even on the days when you are not at the top of your game, then you need scripts!
>
> If you want to be able to provide a tool that new agents joining your team can use to succeed, then you need scripts!

You know, it's interesting that we often get to the point of being "just good enough" in our sales skills and then we stop growing and learning. If you are not selling and listing 100% of your prospects, isn't there still room to grow? Shouldn't we always be striving to be better than our competitors and to exceed our own personal best?

My hope is that, as you read these scripts, you will find them easy and practical, and you will set aside 20-30 minutes a day to practice them and internalize them.

Once you have internalized them, keep practicing until you are flawless, and then keep practicing them as a daily warm-up. Keep them handy for easy reference.

How to Practice

One of the best ways to practice is to find a practice partner(s). I suggest practicing face-to-face and over the phone. When putting your scripts to use, you will communicate with people over the phone and face-to-face, so it is a good idea to practice both.

When you practice, choose a script, eliminate all other chitchat, and get to work. Make the practice sessions realistic. It's okay to hit each other with objections, but don't be ridiculously tough or it will be a negative experience. Make sure to end all role-play sessions with a win. You don't want a negative ending to be stuck in your subconscious.

Continue practicing by going back and forth for the full time allotted, taking turns being the customer and the agent.

Another way to practice is to read the scripts out loud over and over again by yourself. Read them faster and faster, so that when you slow down they will sound smooth and clear.

Some of you will do well when you transcribe them, write them out by hand, or even type them.

If you learn better by listening, then listen to the audio version of this script book over and over again.

A few of my clients have shared their fun and efficient ways of practicing:

1) Practice with their kids.

2) Practice with their team each morning to fire everyone up.

3) Make a deal with their team to hit each other with objections throughout the day to keep sharp.

4) Carry the scripts with them for easy reference, so they can grab extra practice time when they find themselves waiting at the dentist, doctor's office, etc.

5) Record themselves reading the scripts on their smartphone, and then listen to them every time they are in the car.

6) Have the scripts blown up and posted in their office.

7) Say affirmations before their calls and in between conversations. "Prospecting equals freedom," "This is my next appointment," "They really need my help," etc.

Determine what works best for you and do it daily!

Someone shared this quotation with me years ago and I have always remembered it: "Somewhere, someone is practicing, and when they meet you, they will beat you if you aren't practicing harder!"

On the next page I have outlined a few simple communication techniques to give you a head start. For more advanced techniques I encourage you to join our **Speak No Evil Power Persuasion Program**.

Record yourself! You may be shocked to hear how you sound. I challenge you to send a copy to your coach and have them listen too!

Then we will help you fine-tune your skills so that you book more appointments in fewer contacts.

Good luck!

~ Debbie De Grote

President / Founder
Excelleum Coaching & Consulting

Key Communication Reminders

1) Relax and be conversational. If you sound like a telemarketer, they won't like you!

2) Work to build rapport with them as quickly as possible. The fastest way to build rapport is to mirror and match their rate of speech, their tone and inflection, their speech patterns, and their body language (if you are having a face-to-face discussion). If you sound like them, you sound like a friend; if you don't, you annoy them, and subconsciously they identify you as an enemy or a stranger.

3) Key Word Backtracking: As you listen to them you will notice words they like to say a lot—their favorite expressions. Sprinkle them in now and then (it makes them feel like you are talking their language).

4) Acknowledge and Approve: People love it when you are listening to them and they love it when you give them approval, although there is a difference between acknowledging and approving. When you acknowledge, you are saying, "I hear you." When you approve, you are telling them that they are right. Be careful not to get stuck on one or two favorite ways to acknowledge or approve; instead mix it up so that you sound sincere.

Acknowledgement Words:

- Really
- Tell me more
- I'm with you
- I hear you
- If I were you I would feel exactly like you do
- Interesting
- Oh no!
- You're kidding!
- Seriously?
- I can appreciate that

Approval Words:

- Wonderful
- Perfect
- Excellent
- Great
- Terrific
- That's correct
- You are right
- Absolutely

5) When working with prospects and customers, it's critical to ask a lot of questions. However, we don't want to sound as though we are interrogating them. Soften your questions by sprinkling in a few question softeners as you go. You don't need to start each question with a question softener, just a few. You will want to soften the questions that may be more direct or confrontational. "Why" questions can be especially confrontational, so when asking a "why" question soften it with one of the phrases below.

Question Softeners:

- I'm curious
- I was wondering
- Please tell me
- May I ask
- Tell me
- Here's a question

A few additional techniques:

Embedded Commands:

- Hire me
- Choose me
- Meet with me
- List with me
- Sign the contract

Powerful Statements:

- "That's a great question!"
- "That's exactly why we should get together!"

Memory Joggers:

In most of the scripts, you will be asking the client for a referral. Please remember that when they tell you that they don't know anyone, often they just aren't really giving it much thought. To help spark their memory, use memory joggers, like "how about someone at work, church, the kids' sports team, in your neighborhood?" It's amazing that, as you "jog" their memory, they suddenly remember someone.

6) You cannot be powerfully persuasive when you talk fast.

7) Practice the power of pausing. When you pause, it gives them time to catch up. It allows your important thoughts to stand out and sink in.

8) A monotone voice is like a valium. Be interesting to listen to; spark it up, it's show time! This is especially important over the phone, because only 15% of who you really are

reaches through the phone. If the people in your office aren't complaining that you are too loud, you probably need to take it up a notch.

9) Practice active listening. Learn to read between the lines. Listen for their tone and the meaning behind their words. What are they really saying? Take notes. They love it when you write down what they say.

10) Never argue; even using the word "but" is argumentative. Instead use "and yet", "and", or "however". Many of the scripts and objection handlers in the industry are poorly written because they make the client wrong. If you make them wrong, they will naturally shut down and resist you.

11) Avoid weak language. Don't say "if," say "when." Don't say "try," say "do." Don't say "possibly" or "maybe," say "I will."

12) Do not upswing your voice at the end of your sentences. It takes away your power and makes you sound tentative and weak. Practice down swinging your voice at the end, even when you are asking a question.

13) Be an active listener and you will hear everything they say. Don't be quick to accept the "no". Don't take "no" when "yes" is still possible! Simply ask one more question and then attempt to close again. Keep going—take it as far as you can.

Zig Ziglar always said, "Timid salespeople have skinny kids!"

The Listing Success Process

To make it easy for you to study the material, I have outlined each piece of the process, including inserting the scripts and objection handlers where appropriate so that you can follow the flow of an appointment.

Prequalify each appointment thoroughly; ask all the questions!

Even if you know the client and you think you know what they are trying to do or that they will choose you, ask and you won't be blindsided by surprises. If you use the pre-qualification form as a tool/a worksheet, each time you set an appointment, it will help you remember to ask all the important questions. You can lighten up the approach and you can fill in any answers that you already know.

Once the property is listed keep the prequalification form in the file. This will provide your staff with additional information. It will give you something to refer back to as you work on price reductions or offer negotiations in the future.

Setting a Listing Appointment and Prequalification Worksheet

(Print copies of this worksheet and fill it out as you book each appointment. Keep it in a file for future reference)

Client Information

Client Name:
Personality Type:
Address:
Phone Number:
Email:
Preferred method of contact:
Source of Lead:
Date of Appointment:

Questions to Ask

1) Why are they selling?

2) When do they want to put their home on the market?

3) When do they want to be moved?

4) Any special needs or concerns?

5) What they are looking for in the agent they choose?

6) Are there any loans/liens against the property?

7) What do they hope to list their home for?

8) Are they interviewing other agents?

9) Who are they interviewing?

10) When are the other interviews?

11) Is it possible to be the last one interviewed?

12) Does the property have any upgrades or improvement/special features?

13) Are there any repairs or issues with the property?

General description of the property

Beds:
Baths:
Sq. ft.:
Lot size:
Pool:
Other:

Confirm the time and date of the appointment. When you follow up to confirm, do so in an assumptive way: "I am looking forward to meeting with you tomorrow at 3:00 p.m. Are there any additional questions you have before I come out?"

Tell them you will be sending over a pre-listing packet of information (via email or delivery, depending on what's appropriate). Ask for their commitment to review it prior to the meeting.

Script to Set up the Prequalification

"Mr. Seller, my goal is to be extremely prepared for our meeting and to bring exactly what you need from me. To do this, I just need to ask you a few quick questions; may I do that now?"

NOTE: If they say they don't have time, then set a time to call them later. If they don't want to answer a particular question, you can always move on and then come back to it. Usually the more they talk to you, the more they will open up, and you might be able to get the answer later on in the conversation. Whatever you do, don't get into a confrontation over a question they don't want to answer. Move on!

Assumptive technique:

> In preparation for the appointment ask them to have a key and a list of special features ready, as well as any documents you might need.

General description of the property

Beds:
Baths:
Sq. ft.:
Lot size:
Pool:
Other:

Confirm the time and date of the appointment. When you follow up to confirm, do so in an assumptive way: "I am looking forward to meeting with you tomorrow at 3:00 p.m. Are there any additional questions you have before I come out?"

Tell them you will be sending over a pre-listing packet of information (via email or delivery, depending on what's appropriate). Ask for their commitment to review it prior to the meeting.

Script to Set up the Prequalification

"Mr. Seller, my goal is to be extremely prepared for our meeting and to bring exactly what you need from me. To do this, I just need to ask you a few quick questions; may I do that now?"

NOTE: If they say they don't have time, then set a time to call them later. If they don't want to answer a particular question, you can always move on and then come back to it. Usually the more they talk to you, the more they will open up, and you might be able to get the answer later on in the conversation. Whatever you do, don't get into a confrontation over a question they don't want to answer. Move on!

Assumptive technique:

> In preparation for the appointment ask them to have a key and a list of special features ready, as well as any documents you might need.

Assumptive Technique Script

"Mr. Seller, I look forward to meeting with you. When we list your home, I will need to have a key. Could you please have one ready for me, and have it out so that I don't forget to ask you for it? If you have time, would you also be willing to write down a short list of a few special features you especially enjoy about the home, and that you would like me to showcase in the marketing?"

Note: If they say, "I am not sure if I am going to list with you."

"Mr. Seller, I understand, and yet you probably will; most sellers do once they understand everything that I can do for them."

Be sure to use assumptive language—it's not if they list it but when they list it. Speak on the phone and at the appointment as if they have already chosen you. People tend to go with the flow; make it easy for them to move forward.

Send them a pre-appointment package and ask them to review it. This differentiates you from the competition.

Email it, deliver or mail it, and take a copy with you. In a market where properties are selling rapidly, you probably will not want to include the recommended price. You should, however, include a copy of a blank listing contract so that they can get used to seeing it. This is especially good for your analytical clients, who will want to study it thoroughly. This will save you time during the appointment.

You and your team should have a master file and streamlined process, so that they are clear on exactly how to put together a pre-appointment package and listing folder for you. This should include the listing contract, filled out as much as possible and clipped to the inside left of the file, so that it's highly visible when you open the file. Why hide it? They know what you are there to do.

Send them a pre-appointment package and ask them to review it. This differentiates you from the competition.

Script to Prepare Them for the Pre Appointment Package

"Mrs. Seller, to ensure our appointment is efficient and to give you a chance to get to know me and what I will do to sell your home, I am going to send over a packet of information. It will include a market evaluation (what your neighbors have been selling for). Then, when I arrive and tour your home, together we will decide what we feel is the maximum price the home will sell for."

"It is only a few pages, and it will give you a lot of valuable information. Will you take a few minutes to review it before we get together? If, after reviewing it, you have any additional questions or need any other data, feel free to call me."

"Do you prefer that we email it or would you rather we deliver a hard copy?"

"Terrific, we will get that on the way to you today. I very much appreciate the opportunity to work with you and I will see you on _____ at _____."

Script to Be the Last One Interviewed In a Multiple Interview

"Mrs. Seller, I have a business practice. I meet with customers when they are ready to make a decision, so with your permission I would like to be the last one you interview. Also, my clients have told me that they were so glad that they met with me last because I was able to help them compare and make sense of what had been presented. What would be the best day and time for us to meet that would allow you to complete the other interviews?"

"Excellent, I will see you then. Mrs. Seller, I will invest a lot of time to prepare for our meeting. I will be so well prepared that our meeting will only take a few minutes. All I ask is for your commitment that you will not sign with anyone until we have had a chance to meet."

Check the price on Zillow.

Check the price on Zillow before you go, because they almost always will. Even if it's not accurate, you need to be prepared.

Arrive early!

Arrive early enough to drive around the area to scout any listings you may have missed when you ran the data, or FSBOs you did not know about. It is always a good idea to preview the competition, or at least look at the photos or virtual tours online. Google Earth is also amazing. It gives you a great overview of the area from the comfort of your office. Bottom line: however you do it, do your research carefully.

Listings today are goldmines. Don't blow it because you didn't prepare properly!

Arrive on time or a few minutes early; being late is not acceptable. If you are coming from another appointment and are worried you might run late, explain this to the seller and set a 30-minute window. Be sure to be there no later than 28 minutes into the window!

Dress for success.

They are going to pay you a lot of money, so dress sharp. It sets you apart from others and shows respect. Make sure your materials are well prepared and professional.

Be prepared to close them!

Practice your scripts and objection handlers. Have the listing form filled out and ready to go; you can always add price and a few final details at the property. I know some of you like to email them a perfect copy later; that's fine, but get a working copy signed while you are there! Don't leave without a signed contract.

Get your head in the game!

As you drive to the appointment the mental prep should begin. Turn off your cell, turn up music that inspires you, and visualize the sellers signing the contract! As you are walking up to the door, block everything else from your mind and say a couple of affirmations! "This listing is mine!"

Smile!

Act like you are happy to be there, act like you love your job, and show them you are sincerely interested in them.

Open with a strong verbal suggestion.

As you greet them and step into their home, open with a strong verbal suggestion.

Verbal Suggestion Script

"Mr. and Mrs. Seller, I am very excited to be here today and I look forward to getting your home on the market and getting it sold. I am confident that at the end of our appointment tonight you will be 100% convinced that I am the right agent for the job, and will want to hire me to sell your property. Will you follow me through the home and make sure I don't miss any of the important features?"

Note: Why is this important? The human mind runs on a negative track; it is subconscious and we all do it. So that means they will be looking to rule you out. When you plant this powerful and positive verbal suggestion it flips a switch in their mind, and now instead of looking to rule you out they are looking to rule you in. People get what they expect to get. Tell them what to expect!

Look at the home with them.

Take a clipboard or iPad and take notes. They love it when you demonstrate a sincere interest in the property. The walk through gives you a chance to build rapport, ask questions about the home, and gather notes for your suggestions on making the property more sellable.

Bonus Assumptive Technique:

As the seller walks through the home with you, use your smart phone to "record" important details. You can really make it powerfully assumptive by "recording" instructions to your staff. "Mary, when we put the property on the market remind me to be sure to mention X in the remarks." "John, let's be sure to put the sign on the corner of the lot." Remember, people go with the flow; Make it easy for them to move forward!

Avoid detailed discussions about repairs and improvement until you are at the table. The price they want will often help you determine how much they need to do. If possible, avoid the really tough conversations until they have signed the listing. They seem to take the information more seriously once they have hired you. You won't risk offending or overwhelming them with the recommendations, which could cause them not to sign. For luxury properties, you may feel that it's necessary to suggest a home stager. If you have someone whom you trust, and if you are offering this to the seller as a service, pay for the first 1-2 hours. Your stager should give you a discount since you are recommending them regularly.

The Listing Script/At the Table

"Mr. and Mrs. Seller, I have with me the notes I took from our conversation the other day. I wrote down just a few more questions for you. If it is okay with you, can we start with those?"

Reviewing their motivation is a great way to start your meeting off. When you ask questions about things that are important to them it helps to establish a deeper rapport. Use this opportunity to ask any clarifying questions that you might need to ask in order to gain a better understanding of their situation.

Present your marketing plan.

> This is what you will do to sell the home. Due to a large portion of the population being visual learners, you will want to have some colorful pieces to show while talking. You will want to give them a written plan of action. They will love a colorful piece that shows the logos of all of the various websites and partner sites that the property will be featured on.

"Mr. and Mrs. Seller, did you have a chance to review the package that I sent to you? Do you have any questions about the marketing plan included in that package? If you don't mind, let's review it quickly together to be sure you are 100% satisfied with the plan."

"Is there anything else that you were hoping would be done to sell the home that I haven't covered?"

"Perfect, then let's move on to review the market evaluation and determine the price that we should list the property for tonight."

Now it's time to present the Market Evaluation—again.

> Make this as interactive as possible. As you open your folder, the listing agreement should be clipped to the inside left of the folder and the market evaluation, and other documents should be clipped to the right. Make it easy for them to move forward by having the listing agreement filled out as completely as possible. Don't hide it. As you have your discussion, if there is an opportunity to make notes on the contract go ahead and do so, so that you are filling it out as you go.

Script to Review the Market Evaluation

"Mr. and Mrs. Seller, did you have a chance to review the market evaluation that I sent to you? Do you have any questions?"

"Tell me, are you familiar with the other homes that are listed for sale in the neighborhood? How do you feel your home compares to them?"

"Let's review the market evaluation one more time together."

Take them through it, but don't drag it out unless they are analytical. If they are analytical they will naturally want to discuss it in more depth. Once you have finished your review:

"Mr. and Mrs. Seller, now that you have reviewed the facts and the data, tell me, what price do you feel we should list the home for today?"

If you are in agreement on the price, then write it on the contract and sign them up. If you are not in agreement, continue on.

"Tell me, how did you arrive at that number? If you were the buyer and you saw this data, how do you think you would feel about that price?"

"What will you do if the property cannot be sold at this price?" "How long are you prepared to wait to test the market?"

"Did you know that all buyers and agents can see exactly how many days a home has been on the market, and that the longer it has been on the market, the lower the offers usually are?"

"Now that you realize that, I am sure you will understand why our best chance of selling your home at the highest price will be in the first 30 days."

"Our goal is that your property will be the clear choice in the mind of the buyers. To do that, we need to combine my aggressive marketing plan with a price that is accurate and will position your property to sell. The price I recommend is X. Will you allow me to list the property for that price?"

If they say no, and they still want more money, you need to determine if you still want to take it. If you do, then you will want to build in your first price reduction.

Handling Objections

Objections are nothing more than a question in the mind of the prospect.

We have all heard them before, and yet objections still continue to strike fear into the heart of the average salesperson.

While many objections are questions in the mind of the prospect, sometimes they are... ...the customer venting the thoughts that are on their mind....their way of making conversation....a smokescreen for a deeper objection.

...just looking to see if they can shake you up.

Here are a few key points to consider when faced with an objection:

1) Is it an actual objection or is it a condition? You can't eliminate a condition; it is what it is.

2) Is it a serious objection that will potentially require some work to handle, or is it minor?

3) Have they mentioned it more than once? If three times or more, it's likely to be a real issue.

4) What is the underlying worry, uncertainty or belief that is causing them to bring it up, and how can you eliminate it?

5) What is the most practical way to move them forward?

6) What is your attitude as you work through the objection with them? Are you calm, relaxed and open to discussing it, or are you argumentative and defensive?

Remember: they have a right to ask! The more you physically flinch or scowl and verbally react, the bigger it becomes. Answer them as succinctly as possible—sometimes, the more you say, the more objections or concerns you raise. Don't talk so much!

When Handling Objections, Follow This Pattern:

1) When given an objection, take a breath, tell yourself to relax, and allow a pause to show them that you are listening rather than just waiting to talk.

2) Work hard to maintain good rapport with the customer; mirror and match their rate of speech and body language.

3) Repeat back a bit of what they said to show that you were listening and to verify that you understood their objection. Give them acknowledgement and approval.

4) Ask a clarifying question to be sure that you truly understand exactly what they are asking, or what they are really objecting to, before you jump to answer. You may even need to go 3-5 questions deep to really get to the heart of the true objection.

In fact, ask a lot of questions. When you ask questions, it will tell them what direction to take, it will tell you how motivated they are, it will help you get to the truth, and it will help them self-realize that they really do need help.

People don't move forward unless there is some pain involved in staying where they are. The more you can get them to open up to you, the better chance you have of dialing up their pain.

5) Isolate the objection to be sure that it's the only thing in the way.

6) Handle or eliminate the objection.

7) Close.

8) Repeat the pattern as needed.

For those of you who have studied NLP, you may be familiar with a valuable technique called pacing and leading. It actually sounds more complicated than it is.

When you want to lead someone in the direction you know they need to go to achieve the goal they have set, you have to establish good rapport with them first.

In addition to mirroring and matching their rate of speech and body language, you can establish rapport by saying:

"I completely understand why you are asking." "If I were you, I would feel just like you do."

Then you pace, pace, pace. Think of it as though you have met them where they are, and now you are going to step, step, step them away from the objection. Simply make three statements that are undeniably true, and that they are going to agree to without any resistance, whether verbally or nonverbally. Then you will make the leading statement.

Example: "I don't want to sell my home too cheap!" "Mr. Customer, if I were you, I would feel exactly like you do." Pace 1: "I know your goal is to get the home sold." Pace 2: "And I am certain that you want the process to be as painless as possible." Pace 3: "You mentioned that it would be ideal for your family to all make the move together." "Mr. Seller, that's exactly why I am certain you will want to price the home correctly."

Look at how nicely you handled that! Sometimes, by simply meeting them where they are and then pacing and leading them where they need to go, you will persuade them to do the right thing. And we didn't even have to attack the objection, did we?

Remember, your goal is to set the appointment. You don't have to handle every objection on the phone, except those you need to handle to get in front on them!

Don't make them wrong and don't argue—it's not a Ping-Pong match. They are just people; they are not the enemy. They are often fearful and uncertain, and maybe have even had a bad experience in the past. Just go into the conversation with the same approach you would use if they were a friend or family member. Show genuine interest and empathy. Be a real person—the more you sound like a professional telemarketer, the less they will like you!

When my daughters were little, I remember this little book they had. In the story, there was a man sitting on a park bench, and the sun and the wind were having an argument about who could get the man's coat off more quickly.

The wind went first and it blew and blew and blew, and the man clutched his coat even tighter. Then it was the sun's turn, and all it did was shine warmly on the man and he took it off voluntarily. I think of this story often when I am in situations where persuasion is needed to move a customer forward. Don't force it and don't be pushy—just be kind and persuasive.

And keep studying, practicing, and doing more to master it. Let us help you.

Objections at the Listing Appointment

1) Will you reduce your commission?" "I'm curious, why do you ask?" "If I were you, I would ask the same question."

"When you think about it, I am sure you will realize that the commission is really a powerful marketing tool. What I mean by this is when you offer a reasonable rate of commission, it incentivizes my team to work overtime to market your home and it causes the buyer agents to put your property at the top of the list. And that's exactly why we need to list at 6% (or higher)."

"No, I won't pay that."

"I wonder if you have also realized that until I bring you an offer that you are happy with and are willing to accept, and it closes, you aren't paying anyone anything, right?"

"You are the person who decides whether to accept the offer or not, so you actually aren't writing anyone a check today. You are still totally in control. All you're really doing is dangling a marketing carrot."

"There is a saying in real estate: greater exposure equals greater demand, and greater demand equals a higher price."

"Because the commission can impact the exposure and price, I am sure you will want to do the right thing and list it for 6%. It's the right thing to do."

2) "I want to ask for a higher price." "You want a higher price; I do understand that and most sellers feel just like you do."

"And then, just like now, when they see what the market will bear, they realize that they have to price it correctly if they want it sold."

"I know it's hard to find out it's worth less than you hoped for, and because you want it sold and want to move, I know you will see that we need to do the right thing and price it where I recommended."

"No, I don't want to go that low."

"I understand you don't, and I know it is a difficult decision. When you make the decision and we price the home where it needs to be and it sells, and you move on, you will be so glad you did."

3) "I can list high and drop it later, can't I?"

"That's a great question, and if I were you, I would be asking the same thing. Unfortunately, as the days on market increase, the interest and showings decrease. Now that you know that, I am certain you will want to price it correctly so that we can maximize our impact on the market."

"The best chance we have to net you the most money is to price it right today."

4) "I want a shorter listing."

"A shorter listing?"

"Why is that important to you?"

"Mr. Seller, when we list the property, I need to have you under contract long enough to do what we need to do to sell the home for the highest price possible, and the time to close the transaction while you are still under contract with our company."

"Also, we are partners in the process. I am making a substantial investment of time and money and you control the offers you take or don't take. I need to be sure that I have enough time to get you what you need and to get the property sold and closed to get what I need."

"But what if you don't do a good job? I had a bad experience the last time."

"I am sorry you had a bad experience, and if I were you, I would also be concerned about hiring the right agent this time."

"Mr. Seller, if that is what is concerning you, then I would be happy to put an action guarantee in the contract that states that if I do not provide the service that I have promised then you have the option to cancel the listing at the end of the 90 day period. No one ever wants to cancel and so when all is well we can simply continue on together."

5) "I have work to do before I put it on the market." "That's just fine, because you see I have work to do too. Let's do this, we can sign the listing today with a hold do not show until you are ready. This will allow my team and I to have a little extra time to prepare the marketing. Then when you are ready just call me and we can hit the market!"

6) "How many homes have you sold in my area? I haven't seen any of your signs."

"You are right, I have not sold many in your area and that's exactly why you should list with me tonight. You see, I am so excited about branching out to a new area that I am going to work overtime to make a strong impression on you and the neighbors. Also, my company has sold many properties in your area, and I have sold many buyers homes in the neighborhood. When you think about it, I am sure you will clearly see that it's not who has the signs; it's who has the buyers that really matters."

7) "The other agent told me I could get more."

I'm curious, how do you feel about the fact that your price is higher than the data indicates?"
"Do you think they might just be telling you what you want to hear?"

"Mr. Seller, I will always tell you the truth!"

8) "I don't want to list until I find one to buy."

"You want to buy first; I completely understand why you would feel that way."

"May I ask, will you be able to close on another home without the funds from this one?"

"No."

"Mr. and Mrs. Seller, I am sure that you realize that for us to have maximum negotiating power we need to be able to prove to a seller that we are willing and able to close."

"What if we do this, let's go ahead and list the home today, and I will take you out tomorrow and show you some homes so that you can see some examples of what would be available, and then when you feel more comfortable we will go ahead and put the home on the market."

NOTE: If it's a hot market and you know their home will sell easily, if you had no choice you could put a contingency in the listing, contingent upon sellers finding and purchasing a home. It will scare some buyers away and it will be more complicated; however, sometimes it may be the only option.

Things to Think About Before Deciding to Take an Overpriced Listing:

1) How high do they want to go? Set a percentage above the recommended price that you won't exceed, and stick to it. 5% to 10% it depends on your market?

2) Is the property sharp and in a desirable area and price point?

3) Is the motivation strong? They just have a bit of time before it kicks into full gear.

4) Are they reasonable, normal people that you are okay spending some time with?

5) Have you told them the truth?

6) Have you obtained the first reduction, or at least prepared them for it?

The Listing Process Continued

Closing for the signature.

Close them 3-4-5-6-7-8 times. Don't ask them weakly if they want to sign; instead tell them, "Here is what we need to do next". If they resist, take a breath, relax, and ask them questions to determine why they aren't moving forward. Most agents close only once at best, and only a small percentage can close 2-3 times. I want you to be able to go the distance!

Once you find the block, handle it and close again, and repeat until they sign the contract.

If they tell you they need to "think it over", this is not an objection; it is a smokescreen for a real objection. You have to dig it out of them. If they are not making a decision, it is because they are not certain about something. Find out what it is and handle it.

"Mr. Customer, if you are like most people I work with, when they say they have to think it over it is normally because there is something they are still not clear on or still have some uncertainties about. Tell me, what specifically is stopping you from moving forward?"

Sometimes they just won't tell you! Keep digging.

"I do appreciate that it is big decision, so before I leave I want to be certain that I answered all of your questions. So if I may just spend two more minutes to do a quick review."

"Are you comfortable with me and confident I can sell your home? Are you happy with the marketing? Is there anything else you were looking for that we have not discussed?"

"Are we in agreement on the price?"

"Are there any remaining questions or concerns regarding the commission?"

I call this the laundry list. As you go down the list, you will almost always be able to spot the one or more problems. They may not say it in so many words—they may say it more by their hesitation in answering or their tonality. Read between the lines; don't pretend you didn't hear it!

"Mr. Seller, I can tell by your answer that you still have some concerns about X. Let's talk about that."

Now you will work to attack the belief or objection that is stopping them from moving forward. If you have done all of this and they still won't sign, maybe all they need is just a few minutes alone.

"Mr. and Mrs. Seller, let's do this: I have a few calls to return, so let me go do that and give you 10-15 minutes to talk. I will then run back in and see if you have any remaining questions that I can answer before I grab my stuff and take off."

Jump up and go! If you hesitate and wait for them to agree, they may tell you that they will call you later.

When you come back in, be assumptive!

"Where there any remaining questions? No, great! Then all we need to do is simply sign the contract and I will get to work."

If they still say "No", and maybe say, "Wow you are aggressive!"

"Mr. Seller, you are right. I am a salesperson—I get contracts signed, and as much as you may find me a bit aggressive now, if you are like most people you realize that an aggressive salesperson is exactly what you need, isn't it?"

"When you see how aggressive I am when I have a buyer who shows interest in your home you will love me. So let's do the right thing, sign the contract, and let me put all of this energy to work for you!"

If they still won't sign...

Don't leave it hanging. Create with the seller a time when you will call them and when you will see them next. Wrap it up as tight as you can.

If you have to leave them without the listing, leave them with this thought.

"Later tonight as you think about our appointment, the more you think about it the more you will realize that I am the right agent for the job and you will want to hire me to sell your home!"

When you do your follow up do it in an assumptive manner!

"Mr. Seller, I am calling to find out if we can get together tomorrow to get your home on the market and get it sold. Would 5:00 work?"

When you have taken the listing, spend just a few extra minutes to have the price reduction conversation. That will set the stage, in the event that the market rejects the price.

If you are in a low inventory market and it's a price point that is selling quickly, this may not be necessary.

Before you leave the house, ask for a referral. I suggest you create a form to complete in a bright color, and have it in the file as a reminder to you to always ask.

Review your post-listing service plan with them so that they know how and when they will be hearing from you and your team.

This post-listing service plan should be in writing. Remember, under-promise and over-deliver. You must do whatever you tell them you will do! Tell them who is their point of contact on your team and give them their business card.

Give them something that explains what they can do to work more effectively with your team and to maximize showing opportunities.

Some of the agents I coach ask their sellers to describe what type of service and experience they expect, so that the agent can take note of that seller's hot-button service expectations. Then they share them with their team to be sure they are delivered.

When you get back to the office, debrief your team on the needs and wants of the seller.

If you're really smart, you will educate your team on the different personality styles and then note each seller's style in their file.

This will ensure that things go smoothly, and the seller will feel that they have found a home with your team. Work with your team to have understanding rather than judgment when it comes to the customers. We all know that people who are normally very nice can lose their mind when they are under pressure and then become a bit difficult to deal with. Too bad we aren't all buying a new home every couple of years so that we could remind ourselves just how stressful this is for them. Your team should always be gracious, accommodating, and listening for any sign of unhappiness and looking to solve it!

The day after the listing is taken, have your admin or listing coordinator call the seller to introduce themselves and to coordinate any activities, such as inspections, home stagers, etc.

The first week or two of the listing, they will be nervous and will sometimes question whether hiring you was the right thing to do. Put their mind at ease by showering them with extra attention!

You and your team should have a detailed checklist for processing and servicing the listing. Discuss with your team how critical those first few weeks are to build trust and cement the relationship.

A thank-you letter should be sent! In your calendar, choose the day and time each week that you will call your sellers.

If you have too many to call each week, alternate with a staff member and have them assist you, and then call them every other week. If you have a huge listing inventory, you need to call them at least every 30 days, and someone from your team should be calling them each week. I do want to be clear: every 30 days for them to hear from you is not enough, but it is an absolute minimum!

Train your team to be responsive to a customer's emails and phone calls—all messages and emails must be returned, ideally within two hours. Tell them that the day doesn't end until voice mails and emails have been responded to, no matter what. (This applies to incoming messages and emails that are received inside of the business day, 9:00-5:00.)

Themes for Seller Calls

1) Update on the marketing activities you have completed so far.

2) Discuss upcoming future marketing plans.

3) Discuss possible incentives to offer buyers and agents.

4) Discuss upgrades to make the property more attractive.

5) Review how many online hits they have had.

6) Review an updated the market evaluation.

7) Revisit their motivation and time frame.

8) Discuss accessibility if they have not been cooperative.

9) Discuss market statistics—see your monthly MLS report.

10) Review the price reduction plan you created at the time of the listing and tell them that it's time to process it.

11) Offer to show them the competitive properties if needed.

If they won't give you a reduction, consider asking them to extend the listing back to its original term to give you more time. Get the extension, and then go at it again!

To set the stage for this conversation, you will want to update the market evaluation and send them a copy of the marketing plan, noting everything that has been completed and any statistics and feedback that you feel is necessary.

If you feel they will be especially challenging, then have your staff set an appointment for them to come in.

When they come in follow this process.

    a) Verify motivation.
    b) Show them the marketing checklist and that all you promised has been done.
    c) Review the updated market evaluation and any other supporting info.
    d) Show them your next 30-day plan of action.
    e) Tell them what it needs to be reduced to and get their signature.
    f) If they won't sign, get a commitment for when they will.
    g) Repeat this throughout the listing as needed.
    h) As time goes on, if they still won't reduce it then ask them at a minimum for an extension.

i) If they won't do what you ask and they are making you and your team crazy, give it back.

Once it goes under contract, help them understand what to expect from the process.

Shower them again with attention, during the first 2-3 weeks of the pending process, and then be sure to call them each week at a minimum until it's closed. This will insure cooperative sellers and more referrals.

Call and thank them on the day of closing. Talk to them about how you will be staying in contact; ask for a testimonial and ask for a referral.

Make 100% certain that they are added to your database and your follow-up system, and that you have birthdays and all correct contact information.

Depending on the agent on the other side of the transaction, decide if it's appropriate to "adopt the client."

Additional Listing Process Objections

1) "Will you take less commission if you sell it yourself?"

"Mr. Seller, when you think that through, I am certain you will understand that, by reducing my fee, you are really reducing my incentive to bring you my best buyers. In fact, I work with such high quality buyers that some of my clients even offer me a bonus if I sell it myself."

"Remember, you don't write me a check today, so why not give me every reason to show your home to my best buyers? And then, when we have offers on the table, we can take a look at this again if the offers do not net you what you are looking for."

NOTE: If you have to deal with it, you are better off putting it off until there is a contract. Sometimes, once you get past this moment, they never bring it up again.

2) "Will you cut the commission if I also buy from you?"

"Mr. Seller, I cannot do that. I can promise you that I will fight to get the highest price for your home and then work aggressively on your behalf when I negotiate your purchase. When you think about it, just the fact that I am willing to stand firm on the commission shows you how strong I will be when negotiating for you."

"I will protect your money as aggressively as I protect my own."

3) "I need to interview others."

"You want to interview others?"

"Interesting; tell me, what specifically are you thinking they might be able to offer you that I don't?"

"When you thought about listing your home, if you are like most sellers you were probably looking for a powerful agent with a strong track record and an extensive marketing campaign. Mr. Seller, I wonder if you have realized that I am that agent!"

"So when you think about it, there really isn't a need to waste time meeting with others when we can simply sign the listing and get the home on the market today."
"I am already committed; I already set the appointments."

"I can appreciate that you are looking to honor your commitments, and yet if I could share this with you: from a real estate perspective, we seldom have time to even go home and have dinner with our families, so since it's likely that you will choose me is it really fair to waste their time?"

"Here's a thought: I am sure they are decent agents and it would be terrific to have them on our team, so why don't I call them and tell them you have listed with me, and that we would be happy to offer them the opportunity to show the home first, and we will give them half of the commission. This way they aren't angry, we have the best of everything, and we are all working for you!"

"All I need is your signature right here and I will give them a call."

"No."

"Mr. and Mrs. Seller, let's at least do this: let's set a time after your last appointment to meet again for just 10 minutes or so and then I can answer any final questions and help summarize the information."

Script to Obtain Your First Reduction When You Take the Listing

NOTE: Get the listing signed and in your hand first, before you have this conversation!

"Mr. and Mrs. Seller, you have my commitment that I will do everything in my power to sell your property at the price we have listed it for."

"You see, if I do, we all win. You get more money, I get more money. You're happy, and you will use me again and will likely refer customers to me. So you see, I have everything to gain by doing all I can to get you what you want."

"I am sure you understand that the real estate market is unpredictable. So while I cannot guarantee that it will sell for this price, I can guarantee that I will do the activities that I have outlined and will call you often with feedback and recommendations."

"In two to three weeks, we will know where we stand based on the activity and response, or lack thereof."

"Now that you and I are business partners, and while we are here together and have all of this information in front of us, let's discuss what our next strategy would be in the event that the market does not accept our price. If that were to happen, what would you be willing to reduce your price to?"

NOTE: If you can get it in writing on the spot, do it. On some properties you may want to build in 2-3 incremental price adjustments. Even if they won't give it to you in writing, you still win because you have set the stage for that first reduction."

Additional Dialogue:

"Mr. and Mrs. Seller, I am certain you know that most likely our buyer will need to obtain financing. In order to do that, the bank will send out an appraiser who will be reviewing this same data. If the property cannot appraise, then the buyer cannot obtain their financing. This is another reason I am recommending that we list the home for the price of X today."

Price Reduction Objections

1) "I don't want to reduce the price; we haven't had enough showings."

   "Mrs. Seller, if I were you, I would feel exactly like you do. That is why I wanted to share with you that we have had over X number of people view your property on the website, so really, when you think about it, they are online previews."

   "So we have had over X people view the home in person and online and no one was interested in buying it, and that's exactly why we need to adjust the price today."

   "I simply need your permission to make the change; will you give me your permission to do that now?"

2) "You haven't shown the property."

   "You are right; I have been working very hard and prospecting for buyers every day, and yet I haven't found anyone willing to pay the price you are asking. Again, that's why I am calling—we need to adjust the price today, and I recommend we adjust it to X."

3) "Why don't you just do more marketing or have more open houses?"

   "I can appreciate why you would bring this up, and yet I assure you, we have completed all of the marketing activities that we committed to do, and at this point we have massive exposure and still no one is interested. So it's really about the price."

4) "We have a lot of upgrades; our home is special."

   "You are right, your home is special, and that's fortunate because if it wasn't, we would not have had any interest at this price. Luckily, people are interested; they just aren't willing to pay the price you are asking. You see, many of your upgrades are unique and may not fit their needs or their taste."

   "I am sure you can understand that buyers today are not willing to pay over market value for upgrades—it's just not that type of market and economy." "If we want to sell the home, we need to reduce it today by X. Will you give me your permission to process the change today?"

Negotiating Offers With Sellers

NOTE: When you are presenting offers to sellers, think it through carefully and plan your strategy. If the offer isn't fantastic, you may be better off having them come in to the office so that you can sit down with them face-to-face. It's best to bring them to you if possible and get them out of the emotional environment of their home.

Also, it's too easy for them to say no or put you off on the phone, and you may not have the chance to have all parties on the line.

If you know that the offer is lower than they want, don't lead with the price and please don't apologize for the offer. Even if they don't want to take it, they are lucky that someone is interested.

Years ago, I was taught to present offers from the bottom up; tell the clients all of the good things about the offer first and save the price for last.

Once you tell them the price, they don't listen to anything else.

And when you present the price, keep your tone neutral. Just say it, "The price they are offering is X", and then be quiet!

If they react badly, just let them vent. If they get upset that you brought them something lower than what they wanted, try this:

> "Mr. Seller, I realize that this is not the number you were hoping for. Think about this, though: if we are going to be upset with someone, we should be upset with the people who looked at the home and didn't even bother to make us an offer. At least they are making an attempt to work with us. Let's talk about what we can do to put this together."

1) "Can't we counter?"

   > "You can, but not if we want to be sure to sell the house right now. I am sure you know that when we counter we have released them from their contract, and they have to decide all over again if they want to buy it."

   > "If we sign it as is, they have bought it."

   > "Let me ask you to consider this: is it worth risking the sale to see if we can net a couple thousand more? Wouldn't it be better to sign it and sell it?"

2) "Maybe we will get more offers."

   > "Maybe we will; however, at this point, we have been on the market X days and this is the only offer we have had. I wonder if you realize that the longer the home is on the market, the lower the offers usually are."

"Mr. Seller, my recommendation is that we sign the offer and sell the property. It's the right thing to do."

Buyer Objections

1) "I want to work with several agents to get the best deal."

"Mr. Customer, if I were you, I would feel just like you do."

"I am sure that seems like a good strategy, and yet let me share with you an inside-the-industry look at how it really works. You see, to give my clients the time and attention that they truly need, I only work with a few buyers at a time. Most real estate agents will take on as many as they can get, and then they only give their real attention to the buyers that are committed to work with them exclusively. Then they just throw the picked-over leftover properties to the rest."

"As you think about this, I am sure you can see why it makes sense to work with a truly professional agent like myself and have your own representation with someone who is 100% focused on you. And the good news is that you don't even pay for the great services that I provide; the seller pays the commission when you find the home you love."

"You don't have to decide on the phone. Let's do this: why don't you come in and sit down with me, and I will show you the services I provide and all of the ways I will help you beat the crowds to some of the best properties in town, and then you can decide."

"Can you come in this afternoon?"

2) "If I buy from you (the listing agent) will you kick back commission to me?"

"No, I won't do that. What I will do, though, is do my very best to get the home for you. You can imagine that my sellers will be very comfortable with what I recommend because they trust me, so if you are willing to write a reasonable offer and let me help you structure it in a way that I know will make it acceptable, then your best chance is with me."

3) "I want a great deal."

"You want a great deal; can you tell me, what, to you, is a great deal?"

"Is the priority to get something that is just a low price, or are you more interested in finding the home that best suits your needs?"

"If the home is exactly what you want, what is the most you would be willing to pay for it?"

"Do you know what's happening in the market today? Most properties are being sold over asking price with multiple bids."

"If we write low offers, you will lose the property you love." "Let's do the right thing and write the offer at a price that will cause the home to sell."

4) "I want to see more homes."

"Do you want to see more homes because you don't like this one or because you just want to be certain?"

"When you think this through, I know you will realize that this home has everything we have been looking for and it's in the price range that you can afford. I have nothing left to show you."

"It is a great home; let's buy it!"

Or

"Why don't we do this, let's start the negotiations and then when we get the sellers response you will have something concrete to think about."

"No, we still want to think about it."

NOTE: Give them a few minutes let them talk it over. Sometimes that's all they need.

"Mr. Buyer, I have a couple of calls to return; why don't I do that and give you a minute to talk, and then I will come back in and answer your questions before you go."

Be assumptive and positive when you come back in, just like with a listing.

"Now that you have had a few minutes to think about it, let's do the right thing and sign the contract so I can get to work getting the home for you."

"What's the most you are willing to pay to be sure another buyer doesn't get your home?"

(Once they give you a number, ask...)

"If we offer that price and we get a counter offer, will you go higher to avoid losing it?" "How much higher will you go?"

"Shouldn't we just offer that now and put our best foot forward? Then, if you lose it, you will know you did all you could do."

"Why don't we do this, let's start the negotiations and then when we get the sellers response you will have something concrete to think about."

5) "I want to wait until X."

"What is important to you about waiting until then?"

(Is this a condition or objection?)

NOTE: Based on the time of year and the current conditions of your market, you will need to find the reasons that are logical and practical for why they should buy now.

In fact, it would be a great idea to actually create a document:

"10 Reasons To Buy Now"

Remember, since much of the world is visual, if you actually put this in front of them and then explain it, it will have a greater impact.

Remember to dial up the pain. What is the pain they will experience by waiting? Then show them all of the reasons to do it now!

6) "I need to show it to my_____"

NOTE: I hope that you are asking them on your initial buyer consultations if there is anyone else who needs to be involved in the purchase. If they say yes, you get them involved ASAP

However, sometimes it just comes up out of the blue.

> "Tell me, are they going to be involved in the purchase?"

"No, I just need their advice."

> "Even though I completely understand that this is a big decision and I know you are nervous, when you think about it, they really can't make the decision for you, can they?"

> "Ultimately, you will be the one living in the home, and really no one's opinion matters but your own."

> "I find that friends and family members often feel very uncomfortable when put in the position of having to give this kind of advice; do we really want to put them in this position?"

> "I wonder if you recognize just how educated you are now on this market and process, and you have me to help you."

7) "Maybe if I wait there will be more for sale."

> "We don't really need them to tell you what to do, do we?" "It really is okay to go ahead and move forward; let's buy it!"

> "That's possible, and yet we really don't know for sure that there will be other properties that you like as much as this one, do we?"

"It would be a shame to lose it only to find nothing better came along, wouldn't it?"

"Also, I am sure you have thought of this; with low inventory and homes selling so quickly, any future properties will most likely be much more expensive, won't they?"

"Let's do the right thing and start the negotiations today!"

Past Clients and Sphere of Influence Script

Your future depends on the size and quality of your database. If you don't have one, then your number one priority should be to put one together.

Who should be on it? Anyone who knows who you are and what you do: past clients, of course, friends, and family. You may also want to adopt clients on the other side of the transaction.

Look at your phone contacts, your check register, your credit card statements, who you talk to, and who you spend money with, and support them in their businesses.

How to organize it: select a database management program that you are comfortable with, or, if your list isn't big, just organize them in a card file box for now. It's not so much about having a perfect system as it is about having a list, a plan, and a way to organize them that works for you.

As you build your database it will be a constant process of adding and purging. Set a realistic goal of how many you want to add per week. Remember, while we are looking for quantity, we also want quality.

If you have people on your list that you don't like to talk to, delete them or at least move them off of your phone list. If you want to keep them on your email drip or mailing list, that's up to you.

Separate your lists into AAA's, A's, and B's. C's are most likely not people you would call regularly. They might simply be people you have met or would like to meet, and you are contacting them by mail or email.

Your AAA's are your very favorite; 10-25 people who could give you three deals each in a year. Call them every 30-45 days. These are also people you may want to do some extra things for or with; maybe have lunch with them quarterly. Buy them a holiday gift and certainly look for ways you can help them in their business. Set a goal with them of helping you find three deals in the next year. They are more likely to supply the referrals if you set a specific goal with them.

Your Script for AAA's:

> "Hello _____, how are you? Great, I hope all is going well for you. You know I was thinking of you and I just wanted to call and say hello. I also wanted to thank you for your loyalty and support and tell you just how much I appreciate it. If there is ever any way I can be helpful to you in your business, please let me know."
>
> "You know, you know a lot of people, and I was wondering if you might be able to help me with something?"
>
> "Would you be willing to work with me this year to see if you could help me find three great customers to work with? It would be really helpful."

"Thank you so much! I was wondering, can you think of one today, someone I should reach out to who might need to buy or sell or maybe just has some questions for me?"

"Maybe someone at work or church, friends or family?" "Thank you for thinking about it." "I will talk to you soon and please call me if there is anything at all you need!"

Call your A's every 90 days.

Call your B's every 90 days, no less than two times a year.

End of Year Project: At the end of the year, you will want to go through your database notes and look for those who you called and did not speak to throughout the year. Pull those out and, in the month of December, make every effort to talk to them.

Mailings and email are great, and yet, to maintain loyalty over the years and to spark more referrals, they need to hear your voice or see you!

Past Client Script/When it has been a Long Time since Your Last Contact

"Hello_____, this is _____ from _____. How are you?"

"I know it's been a long time since we last spoke, and I just wanted to call today to say hello."

(This is where you will need to do a 15- to 35-second building of the bridge—to do this, ask them personal questions about their family, travels, or job; you need to reestablish rapport.)

Next shift it back to business:

"Have you been receiving my postcards and emails?" "Terrific!"

"You know, I also wanted to apologize for not calling you earlier; are there any real estate questions you might like to ask me today?"

"Today's market is really changing and because of that I will contact you each quarter to give you an update; would that be okay?"

"Great, and while I have you on the phone, is there anyone you can think of today who might need my help?"

"How about you? Are there any real estate plans in your future, in the next year or two?"

"Please feel free to call me anytime if there is anything at all I can do to be helpful to you or your family."

"It's was a pleasure to speak to you today!"

Script For Lead Follow Up

When you are doing your lead follow-up, it's important to be as aggressive about moving them forward as you are when you are prospecting to find them.

Ask questions to determine if this is a valid lead that you should be continuing to follow up with and what follow up plan they should be on.

Leads are only useful if they get you paid. They are not like fine wine—they don't age well—so work to convert them quickly!

You will notice the script for follow-up can be very simple. Think about it; they know why you are calling, so just go for it!

Don't repeat back to them what they have told you in terms of their timeframe, because they may not tell you the truth or the situation may have changed. Ask them again.

A good rule of thumb is this: cut in half whatever timeframe they tell you. It's better to call them more often than not often enough.

Script

"Hello _____, this is _____ from _____. I just wanted to follow up to see if you are still planning to sell your home?"

"I have some time at the end of this week; would you like to get together to talk more about it?"

"Not now."

"When will you be ready?" "What's important to you about that time frame?"

"If you thought you could net more money by selling the house sooner, would you be willing to consider it?"

"Will you definitely put the home on the market in the _____?"

"If I stay in touch with you, would you be willing to meet with me when the time comes?"

If they say they are not sure and sound like they are brushing you off

"Do you even want me to call you back?"

You can use this same script for a buyer; just modify it slightly. Also, you will want to be prepared to sell. Tell them why now is a better time to be selling or buying than waiting. You will want to adjust those reasons to fit the time of year and what's going on in your local market.

If you determine that they are not receptive to you and you are not excited about following up with them in the future, get rid of them. Move them to an email drip campaign and just leave them there. For those of you who have agents on your team, you can delegate the leads that you do not personally want to work. Just be sure that we aren't giving our team members junk that will slow them down.

Script for Asking for Referrals in Social Situations

For a graceful low key way to do this, you simply need to find a way to bring up the subject of real estate. Once you get the topic on the table, they will usually have lots of questions about the market, and then the door is open!

IF YOU KNOW THEM ALREADY: ask how their business is doing. Most people, to be polite, will turn around and ask you about your business. When they do, say this...

> "I am doing well, thank you for asking. And yet it is a challenging market, and I always appreciate any referrals you might be able to send my way. Tell me, who do you know today who might need my help?"

Or

> "You know, business is great, and yet I always have time for another terrific customer. You know a lot of people; can you think of one person today I should be talking to?"

Or

> "It's great, thank you, and the way I love to build my business is by working with the people I know and their friends and family. It's what I enjoy most; do you know anyone today who needs to buy or sell some real estate that might need to talk with me?"

IF YOU HAVE JUST MET THEM: after the introduction and brief chitchat, ask them "Tell me, what do you do for a living?"

Once they answer, you can ask a few more questions about what they do, and almost always they are going to turn around and ask you what you do. When they do, they will most likely ask you how the market is doing. You will want to prepare a simple scripted short answer that is neither too positive nor too negative; something like this...

> "The market is fine; interest rates are low, good homes are selling quickly, and, in fact, we don't have enough homes to sell to all of the buyers we have waiting."

> "Tell me, do you know of anyone who might need to sell or buy that I should talk to?"

> "How about you? Do you have any real estate plans in your near future that I might be able to help you with?"

Another way to open the topic, if you prefer, is to ask them where they live.

> "I'm curious, where do you live? That's a great area; how do you like it there?"

> "You may be wondering why I am asking; you see, I sell real estate and I'm always curious to know what people think about their area."

"How long have you lived there?"

Now you're off and running; they will certainly have questions for you!

When you are wrapping up one of these conversations, your goal should always be to add them to your database in order to build your sphere of influence and referral network.

> "You know, our team sends out some terrific bulletins and updates to our friends, family, and past clients to keep them informed on the market. I would be happy to include you in that information loop, free of charge or obligation of course—just great information. What is your email address? And your phone number?"

Script for an Inside Salesperson to Call Your Database

"Good afternoon, I am looking for _____."

"Hello, my name is _____ from the _____ team, and this is just a quick customer service call. _____ asked me to give you a quick call to see if you have been receiving our mailings and market information. Great!"

"_____ also wanted me to ask if there might be anything at all that you would need to speak with _____ about? I would be happy to schedule a time for them to call you."

"Is there any real estate plans in your future?"

"Also, _____ would love to assist your friends and family if they need some help or have any questions we can answer; can you think of one person today that we should reach out to?"

"Thank you for taking the time to speak with me today. Please feel free to call _____ if there is anything at all you need, and remember, we sell X to X county. Whatever your real estate needs might be, we can help."

Script for the Administrative Team to Ask for Referrals

I realize that most of our administrative people do not like to prospect, and yet if we can simply train them to end each call with this very simple line:

"May I ask you, who do you know today that we could help?"

Or

"We love working with the friends and family of great people like you; who do you know today that we should reach out to?"

Or

"You know, you will be moving soon, and we are going to need another great customer like you to work with. Tell me, who do you know today that may want to buy or sell that we should reach out to?"

Tell your staff that they don't need to be aggressive. Keep it light; we don't expect them to push, just ask gently. You will need to keep reminding them to keep doing it until they create a habit. You may want to reward them for the names they collect, and be sure to stop and thank them each time you hear them asking a client.

Also, remind them that even if they do not collect a name, what they are doing is still very helpful because they are reminding the customers that we need and appreciate their referrals.

P.S. You need to do this too. Do the math—think about the amount of administrative calls you and your team handle in a day over the course of the year. This could be huge!

Script for Asking Your Vendors for Referrals

"Hi _____, this is _____."

"The reason for my call today is to ask for your help. I was thinking about something: you and I have worked together for a long time. As you know, I send you as many referrals as I can."

"As I was thinking about you, I realized that you don't really send me any/many, but it's probably my fault since I haven't asked you to. I wanted to ask, would you work this year to send me at least one referral name per month?"

"I understand that they may not always work out. I will just appreciate that you made the effort, and I will make even more of an effort to send some your way."

"But I work with a lot of other agents."

"I know you do, and that is why I only asked for one."

"Here is what I am going to do: I will send you some of my cards; please send me some of yours. I will also call you once a month to remind us to keep working on this."

"Can you think of one name right now of someone I should contact?"

"Please keep it in mind."

NOTE: They get lazy, and if you don't call them each month they most likely won't make much of an effort. Also, keep a list of your vendors posted and make a note next to their name if they give you a lead. Review the list monthly and call them as a reminder; if they don't try to help, then at the end of 90 days you may want to consider choosing a new vendor.

Script for Asking New Sellers for Referrals

"Mr. and Mrs. Seller, I am delighted that you chose me to list and sell your home, and I want you to know that I will work overtime to do a terrific job for you."

"There is one other marketing strategy that I forgot to mention. I guess you would call it networking."

"You see, every morning I get on the phone and prospect, looking for buyers for your home. As I prospect I talk to a lot of people—some of them are other clients, some are leads, and some are friends and family."

"In those conversations, I am always asking, 'who do you know today who might need my help?'"

"You see, this is how I find great buyers for my listings. Now you are part of this network, and each week, when I call you, I will be asking you the same question."

"So let's start today: is there anyone you can think of who might need to talk to me?"

"Thanks for thinking about it, and if you think of someone later, would you please email their contact information to me?"

Script for Asking a Buyer for Referral at the First Appointment

I have no idea why some of you think you have to wait until the close of a deal to ask for a referral. That's in your head, not theirs. Think about it: while they are shopping for a home, they are obsessed with the task and are likely to be talking to everyone they know about it. This means they are likely to be bumping into others who want to buy too.

This is exactly why you need to start asking for referrals from day one, continue throughout the shopping and pending process, and then for the rest of their life and your career.

"Mr. and Mrs. Buyer, I really appreciate the opportunity to help you find your home."

"I want to let you know, I am going to work overtime to make sure that you have the service you need and end up with the home you love."

"I want you to be so happy that you tell all of your friends about me. In fact, that is how I like to build my business—by working with the friends and family of great customers like you."

"Tell me, who do you know today who might need help buying or selling, or may just have some questions for me?"

"I appreciate you thinking about it, will you keep me in mind?"

"Is it okay if I ask you again?"

NOTE: All throughout the deal, when there is any good news or problems you have solved, ask them again! Your goal is to have extracted two names from them before the close.

If you want lots of referrals, then you need to be dedicated to give great service. Don't drop them when you get them under contract! Stay in touch, make sure to touch base with them at least once a week, and always promptly return their messages to you.

Script for Cold Calls/ Calling Around Listings or Sales

"Hello, my name is _____ from _____. I am calling today because I've just taken a listing in your area over on X. Did you notice the sign?"

Or

"I've just sold a home in your area."

AND

For Just Listed:

"I was wondering if you might have any friends or family interested in looking at the property?"

"How about you, would you like to see it?"

For Just Sold:

"We have leftover buyers and need new listings to sell them; have you, by chance, spoken to any of your neighbors who may be interested in selling?"

"Would you be interested in selling if you knew you could get top price for your home?"

For Either Just Listed Or Sold, continue on:

"I'm curious, how long have you lived in the area? If you were to leave the neighborhood, where would you like to move to?"

"When do you think you might like to make that move?"

"Do you have any real estate questions that I might be able to answer for you today?"

"Just one more question: can you think of anyone at all, maybe at work or church, who might like to sell and might need my help?"

"Thank you for your time! Please feel free to call if there is ever anything I can do for you."

Cold Call Objections

1) "I might sell some day, but I am waiting until X or for X."

"You're waiting until X." "Tell me, why is that date important to you?" "What else are you looking to accomplish by waiting?"

(You are looking to determine whether it is a condition or an objection)

"If you thought you could sell the home now and net more money, would you be willing to consider it?"

"Some people hesitate to put their home on the market until the realize that there really isn't a benefit to waiting."

"When you meet with me, we will look carefully at the market trends and data and, once we do, I know you feel confident that now is a great time to sell the house."

"Let's set an appointment. I will prepare the data so that you can review it and make the decision that's right for you."

"This information will help you set a game plan, and when I leave, you will be well informed."

"It will only take a few minutes, and you will be glad we met!"

"Can I come by this afternoon?"

2) "When I sell, I have someone in mind already that I would go with."

"You have someone in mind?" "I see; who are they? Maybe I know them?"

"I'm curious, are you meeting with them because you are sure they are the most powerful agent you could hire, or simply because you know them?"

"Most people never realize just how much money and time they lost by hiring the wrong agent."

"Wouldn't it make sense to at least have a second opinion? Then you will know for sure."

"I don't think I need it."

"Possibly you don't; most sellers agree, though, that it is truly a good idea to have a second opinion. I would like to see the home anyway, and it will only take a few minutes. Why don't I stop by today?"

3) "If I sell it, I may have someone who wants to buy it."

"You may have a buyer, terrific!"

"I hope that works out for you."

"Tell me, have they signed a contract yet?"

"When will you know for sure if they plan to buy it?"

"Prior to entering into a contract with them, wouldn't it make sense to have a professional evaluation to be sure that you are going to net the highest price possible?"

"I will know in a few weeks and I want to wait."

"Mr. Seller, I'm sure you realize that it would not be unusual for potential buyers in this situation to drag their feet. Them knowing that you are meeting with me may cause them to speed up their decision, one way or the other."

"Also, we can always list it with an exclusion for them, if necessary."

"Let's at least meet and talk about it; it's the best thing we can do to be sure we protect your equity."

"I can come by today."

Script for Doorknocking/ Cold Calling/Farming

"Hello, my name is _____ from _____. I sell a lot of homes in the area and I just wanted to stop by to see if there might be any real estate needs or questions I might be able to assist you with today?"

NOTE: They may ask about the market; have your pre-scripted response ready and keep it short and simple.

"No? Terrific. This is a very popular area, and we always have buyers interested in living here. Tell me, have you spoken to any of the neighbors who might have mentioned that they would like to sell?"

"Thanks for thinking about that. I'm curious, have you lived in this area for a long time?"

"How do you like it here?"

"Have you ever thought of making a move in the future?"

"Really? That's interesting!"

"If you ever were to move, where would your next destination be?"

"When are you thinking you would like to make that move?"

"Why is that time frame important to you?"

"If you thought you could sell your home at a great price, could you make the move sooner?"

"It sounds like you love the area; would you have any interest in purchasing an additional property, maybe as an investment?"

"One more quick question, do you have any friends or family that might need my help? I work a large area and cover X to X county, condo to mansion."

"Thank you, and please feel free to call if you need anything. I am always working and always in the area!"

Script for Telemarketer for Cold Calling

"Hello, may I speak to _____?"

"Hello, this is _____ from _____ at _____ real estate. I am sure you've seen our signs in the area."

"_____ (agent's name) wanted to give you a call today to ask if you might be interested in selling your property."

"You see, we have buyers waiting for homes like yours, and we just don't have enough listings to sell."

"Would you consider selling if you knew for certain that you could sell the home for top price?" "If you ever were to sell, where would you like to move to next?" "Do you have thoughts on when that might be?" "Can you think of any neighbors, friends or family who might need our help?"

"Have you ever thought about buying an investment home or vacation property?"

"We have some helpful real estate bulletins that we send to our clients in the area; would you like to receive them?"

"Thank you for your time today! Please keep _____ (agent) in mind. They are always in the area and they sell property in X and X county, everything from condos to mansions."

Script and Approach at an Open House

When you are holding an open house, think about this: what can you do to stand out and be different from the other agents that they are meeting that same day?

What is it that will cause them to give you their information and/or book an appointment with you?

Ways To Be Different:

Don't just show up at the last minute; plan for this event. Make sure you have a lot of signs placed in the best locations. If possible, knock the area a few days ahead and invite the neighbors. Run a market evaluation on the area so you will be ready to answer questions about value and preview other actives; you might find one that you can sell! Once you arrive, you will of course want to turn on the lights, open the drapes, pick up any clutter and put away any valuables.

How You Should Behave:

- Look sharp—it's really like a job interview, isn't it?

- Stand up but don't pounce on them—let them make the first move. If they offer their hand, great; if they don't, then don't force it. Remember, be versatile; adapt to them.

- Have some helpful and informational handouts. Think of it like your temporary office: you are there to work, not to watch TV, read a romance novel, or chat on your cell phone with a friend. If you do distracting things, you will not be sharp and alert when the customer enters the door. So take work or great sales books and material with you; make good use of the quiet time.

- Smile!

- Be charming and interested in them without being pushy.

- Tell them to make themselves at home; it relaxes them subconsciously.

- Be helpful but don't hover. Give them a bit of space.

- Ask questions in a conversational way that build rapport and gather information.

"Have you seen many open houses today?"

"I'm curious, do you live in the area now?"

"Have you been looking long?"

"What size were you looking for?"

"What questions about this home can I answer for you?"

- ❖ Find ways to highlight the benefits of why they should talk to you and work with you.

- ❖ Find your hook to get them locked in to you! Here's a script that may work for you.

"Mr. _____, tell me, what are you looking for? I might know of something that you might be interested in; I could give you the address to drive by."

"You know, I list a lot of homes and I am often working with sellers who do not quite have their homes ready to put on the market. Let me do this: let me jot down your information, and if I have something coming up, I will let you know before I actually put it in the MLS. This will help you beat the crowd. What is the best number to reach you at if it's really a hot one, and what is your email address?"

"Great! I will keep you posted. You know what else we should do? Why don't we set a time to get together later today or tomorrow? I will show you a few samples of some good matches and you can get a better idea of what your money will buy."

"Then I will have a clearer picture of what you really want, so that when I see it, I can call you and I won't waste any of your time with bad matches."

Your goal should be to get together with them as soon as possible and lock them in to you!

"I am working with an agent." (Maybe they are, maybe they're just trying to brush you off.)

"I see; may I ask, do you have a buyer-broker contract with them?"

If yes, you have to respect that contract and back away; if no:

"Terrific, then you are free to interview me. I have some incredible buyer services that I provide, and they are free to you. My buyers never have to do their own legwork; I do it all for them."

"When can we get together so that I can show you what I can do for you?"

You have your best chance to convert them when you set an appointment while they are there with you!

SUGGESTION: Have some buyer information packages with you so that you can give them some information about yourself and your services to take away.

Follow up with your open house leads that night or the next morning, and keep calling until you reach them. If you don't, someone more aggressive will grab them!

Script for Calling Absentee Owners

"Hi I am looking for _____. Hi _____, this is _____ from _____ real estate. I am calling about your investment property on X street."

"I work with a lot of buyers and sellers in the area, and we currently have an inventory shortage. I was wondering if you would be interested in selling the property if you knew it would sell quickly and at top price?"

"Never, I understand. If I were you I would probably feel the same way."

"Have you owned the property for a long time?"

"Really?"

"I notice you live quite far away (if applicable). Tell me, how did you end up with a property in this area?"

"Interesting; have you ever attempted to sell the property in the past?"

"Tell me, would there be anything that might cause you to consider selling it in the future?"

"If you did, when would that be?"

"Why is that time frame important to you?"

"Would there be anything that might cause you to change your mind and list it sooner?"

NOTE: Sometimes they will ask what it is worth. Be careful; we don't want to get sucked into doing a bunch of market evaluations for unmotivated people. So if they ask you what it's worth:

"I would be happy to prepare a market evaluation for you. May I ask, if you could get the number you want, would you be interested in selling the property now?"

If they say, "maybe," ask them:

"What price would you be hoping to sell it for?"

If they are extremely unrealistic and don't seem to be very motivated, tell them the truth about what the range would be. Based on their reaction, you can then decide what to do with them from there.

"Properties are not selling in that range at this time; if you could not get that price, would you still want to sell?"

"No..."

"I understand. Let me do this for you: I have some important bulletins and information that I send to my clients; may I include you in that list? I will also put in my calendar to touch base with you in 90 days to let you know if there are any changes in the market."

"By the way, would you like to buy more properties in the area?"

"Is there anyone you know locally who might need my help?"

"I have connections with top agents across the U.S. and Canada; do you need assistance with any real estate transactions on any other properties? If so, I would be happy to help you locate a top agent that can help."

"I appreciate your time today, and I look forward to talking to you in the future. If there is ever anything I can do for you, please let me know."

Script for Talking to Renters

"Hello, I understand you are currently renting; is that correct?"

"Tell me, were you aware that, with today's low rates, you can buy a home for not much more, and in some cases even less, than you pay for rent?"

"Has anyone ever shared with you a breakdown of the true cost of home ownership?"

"You see, while interest rates are low, we don't know how long they will stay that way. Also, prices have begun to move up, so if you aren't careful you could be priced out of the market."

"Have you been out looking at any homes?"

"If you were certain that it is possible to buy a great home at a reasonable price, would you be interested in purchasing now?"

If yes, continue. If their answer is no, then stop here and dig in deeper with questions to determine why not. Is it a condition or just an objection? Once you know, you can determine whether it's worth continuing on or not.

"Do you have any interest in buying the one you are living in, if it were for sale? When would you like to be moved into your own home?"

"How much of your savings would you like to invest? Do you have any credit issues or concerns you might need help with?"

"Can I schedule a call for you with a lender who specializes in helping renters buy? Excellent, let's set a time to meet next week once that is completed."

"Also, I would like to send you a home buyer package to help you get to know me and the services I offer, along with some important home buying information. Would you prefer I mail or email that to you?"

"If I need to reach you, what is the best way to contact you, and the best time of day? Do you have any questions or concerns that I can help you with at this time? Terrific! I will have the lender contact you today, and I look forward to seeing you next week."

Script for Expireds

"Hi this is _____ from _____. I am calling to find out if the house is still available for sale."

(If they say yes, it may be relisted or they may not know it has expired, so probe further.)

"Great, I will make a note of it. Tell me, is your real estate company still _____ and is your price still _____?"

(If they say no and tell you they are now with a new company, you will know they have relisted it. Thank them and move on.)

(If they say yes, and it is with the same company and listed at the same price, you need to verify to see if they relisted.)

"Interesting, because you know the MLS shows that the property is expired. Have you relisted it?"

"No."

"Did you know that it expired last night?"

"Did you still want to sell it?"

NOTE: If they say no, don't assume they are telling you the truth. Remember, you are a stranger and they are likely unhappy with agents, so why would they volunteer information? Keep digging in a curious and interested manner.

"Really? I'm curious, why not?"

"When you had the home on the market, where were you hoping to move to?"

"If you could sell the home, would you still like to make the move?"

"Did your agent tell you why the home didn't sell?"

"Why do you think it didn't sell?"

"The market, the price, etc."

"Really? Did they explain that there are many factors that may cause a home not to sell?"

"You see, while what they told you may be true, it may not have been the main reason or the only reason. And once you discover what really got in the way, we could correct it and then the property would sell. That's exactly why we should get together!"

"Why don't we do this: I will be in your area today, and I would like to see the home. Let me pop in for five minutes, and I will take a look and I will tell you the truth about what I think may have stopped it from selling. Can I stop by around 4:00?"

If they say "Yes, but I am not listing."

"I understand, and if I were you I would feel exactly like you do. And when you think about it I am sure you will realize that you have nothing to lose by having me take a quick look; how about 4:00? Will that work?"

If they say "Okay", try to go a bit further.

"You know, since I will be stopping by anyway, why don't I do this for you: let me run an updated market evaluation for you. I will also bring information on what I do that causes my listings to sell and causes them to sell for top price; I am sure you will find it helpful."

NOTE: If they say they aren't listing and don't need it:

"I know you don't plan to list now; however, won't it put your mind at ease to finally know what caused it not to sell, to know exactly where you stand in the market, and to know that there is hope? And that when you need it, that there is a plan that can get the job done for you?"

"It will only take about 10 minutes, and the more you think about it, the more you will realize that you have nothing to lose by meeting me, do you?"

"Does 4:00 work, or is there a time that would be better for you?"

NOTE: When you get there, go for it! I realize that this is not a qualified listing appointment in the sense that they told you they were listing. Think about this, though:

They wanted to sell, they tried to sell, they were willing to hire and pay an agent, and they have just agreed to meet with you. Unless you are already busy with back-to-back appointments, wouldn't it be worth it to get in front of 2-3 of these people a day, or even a week? Also, you will find that it is always easier to build rapport face-to-face and much more difficult for them to be tough when you are standing in front of them smiling.

NOTE: What if they say they want to sell but they don't want to list, and they ask you "do you have a buyer?" DON'T TELL THEM YOU DO IF YOU DON'T!

"You know, _____, we (you, your team, your office) have many buyers we are working with; however, I wouldn't want to mislead you and tell you that I have a buyer when I am not sure that I do. Once I see the home, I will be able to tell you if I do or don't on the spot. Can I come see it today at 4:00? I will be in the area anyway."

NOTE: If you do find that you have a buyer, get something in writing agreeing to price and commission before you show it!

"I don't think I will be selling; I just need a break."

"I understand. You must be tired of this whole process. Let me ask you one last question if I may: over the next couple of months, if I happened to come across someone who I felt would be right for your home, would you want me to call you?"

"Yes."

"Okay, I would be happy to do that. I will keep you on my inventory list."

"You know, I don't like to waste your time, and that's exactly why I should take a quick look at the home. That way I will know for sure if any buyers I meet are truly a good match, and if they aren't, I won't bother you. Again, I am going to be nearby; can I just stop in for a quick peek?"

NOTE: If an expired hangs up on you quickly into the conversation, call them back the next day or the day after that. You don't have to remind them that you called the day before; it's unlikely they will remember you. Just start over. It's amazing what a difference a day can make.

NOTE: If they say they want to sell, are interviewing agents, and already have their interviews set or already have their agent chosen, have your statistics ready!

Prove to them that you are someone worth meeting with, and don't give up easily.

Example: "Mr. Seller, did you know that the average agent sells only 4 homes a year? I will sell X this year. The average agent sells only 75% of what they list, and I sell 99%. The average agent's days on market is 67, while mine is 22, and the average agent sells their listings for only 90% of list price, while I sell mine for 96%. So not only do I sell more houses, I sell them in less time for more than 6% of what other agents can do."

"Because you can see now that I am different, I am sure you now realize that this is exactly why we should meet."

"When is your last interview? Let's schedule a time now for me to come in after they do."

You must be able to explain clearly why you are different in 55 seconds or less.

Expired Objections

1) "I am relisting with the same agent."

   "Interesting; so you are thinking of giving them another chance?"

   "You know, Mrs. Expired, I understand that they are most likely pressing you to renew with them."

   "I would imagine that, since you are going back with them, you must think they did all they could do the last time?"

   "I am sure they called all of the prospects and leads they had."

   "Because they have already done everything they know to do, and called everyone on their list to call, I am sure you are wondering what will they really do differently for you this time that they haven't done already. That's exactly why it makes sense to meet with someone who can offer you a new plan, like I can, doesn't it?"

   "Let's do this: let's set an appointment for today, and in a few brief minutes I can show you what I do differently that will get your home sold!"

(If they still resist, this is where it would be a good time to use your stats!)

   "Mrs. Seller, sometimes people hesitate to meet with me until they discover the results my marketing campaign creates."

   "You see, I sell over X number of homes per year. Did you know the average agent sells less than 4 per year? Also, I sell 95% of the listings I take, while the average agent sells only 75%, and I sell my listings for 98% of list price, while the average agent sells theirs for 95% of list price. I typically sell them in less than 3 weeks; the average agent takes 2-3 months.

   "So not only do I sell many more homes, I net my clients more money and I do so in a fraction of the time."

   "After we meet, you will be 100% convinced that I can do the same for you!"

   "Let's set a time for today; you will be glad you did."

   "How about 4:00 today?"

If they still resist:

   "Mrs. Seller, when I list your property, I will provide a written plan of action and an action guarantee. I will also look at your property and share with you exactly what might have gone wrong, as well as what can be done to make sure the sale is successful this time."

"Once you review the plan, you can decide if you want to list or not."

"I am going to be in your area anyway; why don't I stop by for at least 10 minutes?"

2) "I am going to wait/take a break."

"You want a break?"

"I can imagine you are really tired of this whole process; I would feel the same way if I were you."

"Tell me, when you had the home for sale, where were you planning to move to?"

"Is that still something you would like to do?"

"When would you like to be there?"

"Would you still like to sell the home if you could?"

"You have probably thought about this: we really only need one right buyer for your home, and wouldn't it be a shame if that right buyer came along and your home wasn't for sale and they missed it?"

"Yes, but I don't want to list it."

"Mr. Seller, I can appreciate that you are discouraged. Let me ask you: did your agent tell you exactly why the house didn't sell?"

"Price/market conditions."

"Well that could be true. Did they tell you, though, that there are many factors that can cause a property to not sell?"

"No."

"Really? That's interesting. You know, I am going to be in your area this afternoon. Let's do this: why don't I stop by and take a look at the house with you? Within a few minutes, I can tell you exactly what caused it not to sell. I will also do a bit of research before I come to see how the marketing was handled, and I will pull up the current comparables."

"After we spend just 10 minutes or so together, I will be able to tell you exactly what will need to happen for it to be sold, and I can show you how I can help."

"Will 4:00 today work?"

"No, I just want to wait."

"You know, Mr. Seller, most expired sellers say the same thing until they realize that they have nothing to lose by meeting with me, and that, if nothing else, it will give them peace of mind to finally know what really went wrong."

"Because I know you must be wondering what really happened, I am sure it will be worth your time to let me stop by."

"What time today would be better for you?"

"No."

"Okay Mr. Seller, I understand. Before I let you go, may I ask just one more question?"

"If I were to come across a potential buyer for your home, would you still like to show it and sell it?"

"Yes."

"Great! I will keep you on my inventory list and call you if I feel I have a match. I don't like to waste anyone's time, so since I will be in the area anyway, would it be ok if I just take a look, so that if I do call you with a buyer I will know it truly is a good match?"

Now at least you're in. By now you should have had enough conversation to know whether or not this is one worth getting in front of. If they seem reasonable and the property seems good, go, and when you go, you are going to list it! So once you are there, go for it! If you can't list it while you are there, your goal is to convince them to set a listing appointment in the near future.

3) "I am going to try it on my own."

"So you are thinking of doing a For Sale By Owner?"

"I see."

"May I ask, what caused you to decide to sell it on your own?"

"I had a bad experience, I don't think agents do very much, etc."

"I am really sorry to hear that!"

"I have talked to other For Sale By Owners who felt the same way you do until they met me and realized that I am different. I am confident that when we meet, you will feel the same way they do."

"Why don't we do this: I will be in the area this afternoon; why don't I stop in and you can show me the home?"

"I can be there by 4:00."

4) "I already have my interviews set up with other agents."

    "Okay, so you have scheduled interviews. Good for you!"

    "Tell me, how many people have you scheduled to meet with?"

    "I see."

    "May I ask, how did you choose them?"

    "You know, Mrs. Seller, prior to meeting with me, other clients also felt they needed to interview other agents until they reviewed my track record and marketing campaign."

    "When you think about it, why not meet with just one more agent, especially one like me who has sold (add your stats here)?"

    "Let's go ahead and set a time to meet; I know you will be glad we did!"

5) "I don't want to drop my price."

    "So you would like to keep the price the same."

    "If I were you, I would feel exactly like you do, and yet you had the home on the market and you clearly would still like to move. I know you realize that price could be a factor."

    "Did you know, Mr. Seller, that there are also a number of other factors that could have caused the property not to sell?"

    "Let me ask you this: if you could get the home sold at a fair price, would you still like to move?"

    "When the home sells, what are your plans?"

    "Would it be a problem for you if the home sold in the next month or two?"

    "To get the home sold and be done with all of this, what do you feel is the lowest you would be willing to go?"

    "What will you do if you find that you cannot get the price you want for the home? What are the other options you might be considering?"

    "Did you have any offers when it was on the market?

    "You know, it sounds like we really should get together. I know that I can help you!"

    "Because, you see, while it may have been the price, it could have been something else that stopped it from selling. When I stop by, I will bring updated comparables and I will tell you the truth about the price. Then we can go from there."

"Would today work for you, or would tomorrow be better?"

"I don't have to sell."

"You don't have to sell, good for you!"

"Tell me, when you had the home for sale, where were you planning to move to?"

"Have your plans changed?"

"I'm curious, what are the other options you are considering?"

(They may say that they want to keep it or wait; if so, go back and review the dialogue we just covered. If, however, they say they could rent it, see below.)

"If you thought you could get the property sold rather than renting, would you prefer to do that?"

"Do you own other rentals?"

"Have you discussed how renting it would impact your capital gains situation with your CPA?"

"Would the rent cover the payment and expenses?"

"How long would you hold it as a rental before you would try again?"

"I wonder if you realize that most tenants will not maintain the property well, and you may be faced with expensive repairs when you are ready to sell."

"I am sure you know that, in today's economy, it's not unusual to have trouble with tenants paying on time."

"If you had to come out of pocket with money to cover loss of rent or repairs, how would that impact you financially? Could you do it?"

"If you knew for certain that you could sell the property at a reasonable price and be done with it all, wouldn't that be a better option?"

"I have a suggestion: let's set an appointment, and I will sit down with you so that we can look at all of the facts and all the options to see what truly makes the most sense."

"Even if you decide not to list the home, at least you will be well-informed. We can stay in touch and I will be there to help you in the future."

"I can come by today; what time is best for you?"

Script for the For Sale By Owner

"Hi, I am calling about the house for sale; is it still available?"

"Great."

"My name is _____ from _____, and I work in the area. I was wondering, what are your plans for the property if you are unable to sell it on your own?"

"Will you be interviewing agents?"

"How long will you try it on your own before you would consider listing?"

"Are you cooperating with agents now if they have a potential buyer for the property?"

NOTE: Many will say yes.

"Obviously you are open to working with agents, and because of this, wouldn't it make sense to meet with a local professional like myself to explore what I could do for you?"

"Not yet. I want to try it on my own to save money."

"If I were you, I would feel exactly like you do. Tell me, where are you hoping to move to?"

"What is your timeframe for making the move?"

"When you think about the fact that you are looking to sell the home for top price and net the most money, it does make sense for us to at least meet, doesn't it?"

"I will be in the area this afternoon; may I stop by, see the property, and spend just 10 minutes with you?"

If they say yes, you want to set the stage to have a chance to sit down with them.

"Terrific, I will look forward to seeing you then. And as a way of thanking you for meeting with me, I will bring you an updated market evaluation and a copy of my marketing program, what I do to get homes sold. If you have just a few extra minutes, I will quickly walk you through both."

If they say, "I don't need your marketing plan; I am not listing."

"I know, that is what you said, and yet wouldn't it be helpful to have ideas from a professional? Who knows? You might find something you can use now as you work to sell the home on your own."

"Also, wouldn't it be nice to have a plan B, just in case you cannot sell it? Then you will know who to call."

"I will see you this afternoon."

NOTE: When you get there, avoid what I call "hallway presentations". What I mean is this: don't let them pick all the critical information out of you in the hallway.

Instead, tell them that you are happy to answer all their questions and ask to sit down with them for a few minutes. Then go for it!

Since this is not the type of appointment where they are telling you that they are going to list, you may be thinking, "should I go on these?" Again, that depends on your schedule and your prospecting plan. Think about this, though: they want to sell, they are trying to sell, and you know what they are asking. I am hoping that, through your questioning and conversation, you have determined that they are motivated and somewhat realistic.

The only thing stopping them from listing it is that you need to go convince them!

Script for New Buyer Agents to Use When Calling FSBOs

Maybe you are too busy to go out on FSBO leads, and you have a buyer agent who may not be super skilled or super aggressive. That's okay; get them out there meeting the For Sale By Owners. If there are a lot of FSBOs in your area, you may want to do the FSBO previews in a 10-minute radius around your office and only see the others if they are serious about listing.

Why this is such a great idea?

- They should be previewing property anyway.
- It gives them practice talking to people about real estate.
- It's easier for them to sell you to the customer than it is to sell it themselves.
- You have a track record that they can promote!
- They can prescreen them to eliminate the strange, ugly, and unmotivated and just bring back the hot ones!

Give them this simple script, set a goal of how many you want them to see each week, and give them a few of your prelisting packages to take along. To keep it simple and affordable, you may want to create an 8 x 10 sheet with your bio on the top half and testimonials on the bottom half. This would be easy for them to leave behind.

Script

"Hi, I am calling about the house for sale."

"Hi, my name is _____, and I am a buyer's agent at _____. I am planning to be in the area today previewing properties; may I look at yours?"

"I am not interested in listing."

"I understand, and I don't even take listings since I am a buyer's agent. May I stop by?"

"Do you have a buyer?"

"We have several buyers that we are working with, and I won't know whether I have a buyer that is right for your property until I see it. I will be in the area around 4:00; can I pop in then? Would that be okay?"

"Yes, but I am only paying X%"

"I will make a note of that."

Once they are at the property, the buyer's agent's job is to ask questions, build rapport, and determine whether or not it's one you would be interested in listing. If it is a good possibility then they can use the script below.

>"Mr. Seller, you should meet my senior associate. They sell so many properties, and I know they could help you. Can I set a time for them to come and see you/call you?"
>
>"You know, I have a little information about them with me; may I leave that with you?"

When they return to the office, have them give you a quick run down of their visits so that you can determine the follow up plan that's right for each FSBO.

Effective FSBO Follow Up

For FSBO follow-up to be effective, it has to be consistent and direct. They know why we are calling, so just get to the point! The best time to follow up is Monday, or anytime you do it!

"Hi, it's _____ from _____. Remember me?"

"Great! I was just calling to find out if you sold the property?"

"No!"

"Really? Well then it's a good thing I called. I am going to be in the area today; why don't I stop by and list it for you, and then you can take next weekend off?"

Or

"Hi, it's _____ from _____. I was just following up with you again; did you sell the property yet?"

"Oh that's too bad. You see, since we last met, I have sold X homes and I would love to have yours be next. Why don't we get together today and talk about it? I can stop by at 4:00; will that work for you?"

Or

"Hi, it's _____ from _____. I was just checking in to see if you are ready to list the home. I know that my aggressive marketing plan will be exactly what you need to get it sold. Let's do this: let's get together and talk about it. What would work best for you?"

FSBO Objections

1) "I have sold others before. I can do it on my own; I don't need you."

"You have sold others, terrific! It's a pleasure to talk to someone who actually knows what they are doing!"

"It sounds like a very nice property; I imagine you can find a buyer."

"Mr. Seller, here is a thought: if you can find a buyer with the limited exposure you are able to provide, can you imagine how many buyers I could deliver with my professional and aggressive marketing campaign?"

"I will be in the area today. May I stop by and see the home, and take 10 minutes to show you what I can do for you? What time would work best for you?"

"May I ask, if you were unable to sell the house on your own, when would you be thinking of listing it?"

"Not for a while or not at all."

"One more quick question: are you cooperating with agents if they have buyers for the home?"

"You know, Mrs. Seller, I have many buyers that I am working with. I am not sure if I have one just right for your home; may I come and take a look?"

"Excellent, I look forward to meeting you. You know, since I will be stopping by anyway, why don't I do a couple of things for you? I will run a quick updated market evaluation and bring that in for you, and if you have just five extra minutes, I can review all of the things that I can do to sell your home for the most money possible."

"But I am not listing."

"I know, that is what you said; however, when you see what I can do for you, I believe you may want to change your mind. And even if you don't, I know I can leave you with some good ideas that may help you sell the home yourself. If something that I share with you works then maybe you will send me a referral, so we really have nothing to lose, do we?"

"Great! Let's meet this afternoon."

2) "I had a bad experience with a realtor last time."

"Wow, a bad experience. That's too bad!"

"I can understand why you would be hesitant to try again."

"I am sure you realize that, in any industry, there are top notch professionals and there are those that aren't so good. I am one of the good ones, and when you meet with me, I am confident that you will realize just how different I am."

"Why don't I stop by and spend just a few minutes with you? If nothing else, at least I can be helpful and show you that we aren't all bad."

3) "I have a lot of interest already."

"A lot of interest, that's great!"

"I'm curious: is the interest primarily from buyers or other agents inquiring about the home?"

"Both, good for you! How many showings have you had?"

"Really, only that many? How many offers?

"None? Oh, that's not good, is it?"

"It sounds like it's a good thing that I called. You see, I specialize in working with For Sale By Owners, and I know that I can be of help."

"Let's set an appointment so I can show you exactly what I can do to sell your home for top price in the shortest amount of time possible, with the least amount of stress."

"I can be there in an hour; will that work for you or do you prefer later in the afternoon?"

4) "I don't want to pay a commission."

"I see. You are trying to avoid paying a commission."

"Other For Sale By Owners have also said that before they realized that, with the massive exposure that I can provide that often sparks multiple bids, I really end up paying for myself."

"After you meet with me, you will be totally convinced that it makes sense to hire a professional."

5) "I am a salesperson. I sell X (cars, etc.).

"You're a salesperson, terrific! What do you sell? Really? How's business?"

"I wonder, since you are an expert in your field, if you have thought about how it would make sense to hire someone who is an expert in selling property?"

"I can handle it myself."

"You know, Mr. Seller, it sounds like you have a good property and you are a smart person, so I would imagine you may be able to find a buyer. I also wonder if you have thought about this: if you can find a buyer, how many more buyers would a full time professional like myself be able to bring you?"

"You know, many of my properties receive multiple bids, and by the time the negotiating is done, they end up with more than they ever thought possible."

"I have a saying: maximum exposure equals a greater demand, and a greater demand nets you a higher price."

"Let's do this: let's get together, and I will prove to you all the ways that I can increase the exposure for your home."

"If nothing else, you will pick up some great ideas and I will get to see the home."

6) "I used to sell real estate."

"You used to sell real estate! Awesome! Where did you work?"

"Interesting; how long ago was that?"

"I can understand why you thought you would try it on your own."

"You might find yourself wondering, though, if it would make sense to just go ahead and turn it over to an active agent who specializes in your area and has an aggressive plan."

"I would really enjoy meeting you, and I know that you will gain a lot of valuable information from the meeting. Let's get together today, and I will show you what I can do for you that is different."

"What time can I stop by today?"

7) "I am going to try it on my own for X."

"I can appreciate that. It sounds like you must have a little time."

"May I ask, where are you moving to?"

"When would you like to be there?"

"How long will you try it on your own before you considering listing it?"

"When will you begin to interview agents?"

"You know, here's an idea: I would like to see your home, and you may eventually need to hire an agent, so we should meet so that I can see your home and show you what I do that causes my listings to sell for more money and in less time than the average agent. I can be there in the next two hours; will you be home?"

"Yes, but I don't want to list."

"Sometimes clients say that, and sometimes they end up listing and sometimes they don't. Either way I would like to see the property."

"How about today at 4:00?"

Script to Thank the Customer At or After Closing

"Mr. and Mrs. Customer, I just want to say thank you! I know there are a lot of realtors out there and I really appreciate that you chose me."

"I hope you were happy with our service."

Allow a pause and let them tell you. If it's a no, don't be defensive; just listen and tell them you appreciate their honesty and that you are committed to correcting the issue.

"Yes."

"I am glad you were happy with our service, and I want to give you my commitment of continued service. I will stay in touch with you by mail and email with important market updates, and I will call you quarterly to see if you have any questions. Will this be okay?"

"Excellent."

"Of course, I hope that you will feel free to call me anytime now that your deal is closed. I need another great customer like you; tell me, who do you know today that I should talk to?"

"Thank you for thinking about it, and you know I always appreciate your referrals."

"May I ask you for one small favor? Would it be okay to use you as a reference? Thank you for that, and would you mind writing just a short testimonial for me?"

"Or, if you are too busy and would be willing to give me a quote now, would it be okay for me to write it down and use it in printed materials if needed?"

"Thank you again, and I will check in with you in the next month to be sure everything is going well."

Script for Asking a Buyer to Work Exclusively With You

Before a buyer commits to working with you exclusively you will probably need to spend time with them; building rapport and taking them through the needs and wants portion of the consultation.

Once you are clear on their motivation and needs, you will want to spend a few minutes explaining to them what you are going to do for them, as you work with them to find their home.

Create a bullet pointed plan of action or your "Home Buyer Search Services" and review this with them.

Next, it's a very easy transition to ask for their commitment to work exclusively with you.

"Mr. Buyer as you can see there are many services that I provide as we work together. I truly leave no stone unturned to find a home that you will be happy with."

"The great news is that all of these services are free to you (other than some rare exceptions) I get paid by the seller when I find the home you love."

"All I am asking for is simply this, your commitment to work exclusively with me to find the home you love; may I have that commitment?"

NOTE: If you are using a buyer broker contract the wording would be only slightly different.

"All I am asking for is simply this, your commitment on this very standard buyer broker agreement to work with me exclusively for a period of X. Will you sign here please?"

Script for Asking the Buyer to Start the Pre-Approval Process

"Mr. and Mrs. Buyer, as you know an important piece of the home buying process is obtaining your financing."

"I am sure you are well qualified, and because of that we will want to be able to prove this to any sellers we are negotiating with by providing a letter of pre-approval."

"In fact, some listing agents and sellers won't even open negotiations until they have proof of your qualification in their hand. That's exactly why we need to get you together with a lender and begin the process."

"Because you two are the type of home buyers who want to be well prepared and well informed I know you will want to get this handled right away. When, in the next day or two, can we get you together with the lender?"

Great FSBO Questions

1) Will you be interviewing agents soon?

2) How long have you been on the market?

3) Do you have any offers pending?

4) Have you had a lot of activity?

5) What are some of the things you have been doing to market the property?

6) I'm curious, which of those activities are bringing you the best results?

7) How long, do you think, will you try it on your own before listing it?

8) Would you be open to a 2nd opinion?

9) I'm curious, what was the main reason you decided to try it on your own?

10) Are you cooperating with agents if they have a buyer?

11) May I keep you on my active inventory list?

12) Do you have any specific terms/time frame/price that you are looking to accomplish?

13) Would you consider listing the property if you knew for a fact that I could provide the exposure you need to net top dollar?

14) May I come by to see the home and to show you what I can do for you?

15) Wouldn't it be nice to have a backup plan just in case you find that you need it?

Great Questions to Ask Expireds and Old Expireds

1) When do you plan to put the home back on the market?

2) When you had it for sale where were you moving to?

3) What happened?

4) Would you still like to move there if you felt you could get the home sold for top price?

5) Did you know that inventory is much lower than when you tried to sell it before?

6) What do you think your agent should have done for you that they didn't do?

7) What reason did they give you for why they weren't able to sell it?

8) Did they sit down and explain all the additional reasons that might have stopped it from selling?

9) When do you think you will try to sell it again?

10) How would you select the agent you would work with?

11) What questions do you maybe have about the market that I can answer for you?

12) Can we schedule a time, and I can look at the home and give you my honest opinion of what went wrong and what it would take to get it sold?

13) Wouldn't it make you feel better to have clear answers and information?

14) When you think about it you really have nothing to lose by meeting with me do you?

15) Can I come today at…or tomorrow at…?

Resort Script:

"Hello Mr. _____. My name is _____ from _____."

"I am calling about your property on _____. The resort market is improving and I was wondering, do you have any plans to sell the property?"

"Are there any questions about what is going on in the local market that you would like to ask me?"

"I'm curious, do you live in the property full time or is it a vacation home?"

"How long have you owned it?"

"How did you happen to purchase a property here in _____?"

"Would you be interested in purchasing something else in the area?"

"Do you have any friends or family who may have an interest in purchasing something nearby?"

"Would there be any chance that you might want to sell the property at some point in the future?"

"When do you think that might be? Why is that time frame important to you?"

"If you were to sell do you have someone in mind that you would work with?"

"If I stay in touch with you and keep you up to date on the market prices and conditions, would you allow me to help you when that time comes?"

"Terrific what is your email and primary address so that I may keep you in my information loop?"

"Is there anything I can do for you today?"

"What I will do for you, with your permission, is touch base with you at least 1-2 times a year to give you a market up date; will that be ok with you?"

"Excellent, I will send you my contact information today. Thank you for your time."

Promise Technique

The promise technique is one of the most valuable and under-utilized techniques and it's so simple. When you want to cement an agreement simply ask them to "Promise You." When people make a promise most will work to live up to that promise.

EXAMPLES: When a seller tells you I can't list now, but I will list with you when I am ready.

"Mr. Seller I look forward to working with you...so when you are ready you promise to list with me correct!"

When a buyer tells you they will be loyal:

"Mr. Buyer I am confident that I can find you the home you will love and I will work overtime to do so, in exchange I have your promise that you will work exclusively with me right!"

When calling a past client:

"Mr. Past Client I appreciate you and your loyalty, I will do everything I can do to be of assistance to you and your friends and family whenever you need me. In return, will you promise me that when you buy or sell, or know someone who needs to buy or sell you will call me?"

Always thank them for their promise to further cement it, and if they are face to face with you shake their hand to lock in the promise.

CPSIA information can be obtained
at www.ICGtesting.com
Printed in the USA
BVHW010613130419
545428BV00003B/4/P